MODERNIQUE

MODERNIQUE

INSPIRING INTERIORS MIXING VINTAGE AND MODERN STYLE

Julia Buckingham

WRITTEN WITH JUDITH NASATIR

PRINCIPAL PHOTOGRAPHY BY ERIC HAUSMAN

ABRAMS, NEW YORK

FOREWORD

Juxtaposition has long been considered the judge and the jury of great design and good taste.

It is within this masterful mix of the old, the new, the rustic, and the refined—with a healthy dose of absolute audacity creating the unexpected—that I find the most interesting of ideas manifest. It is within this madcap mashup of contradiction that Julia Buckingham finds her inspiration for *Modernique,* always achieving a surprisingly superlative outcome of uncomplicated style. Her design sensibility has always captured my imagination, igniting, enticing, and exciting my eye! Julia Buckingham has always had my attention.

It's not by happenstance that our paths would cross. Like me, Julia has had an unwavering eye for beauty since she can remember remembering. Julia and I met early in our careers at Neiman Marcus, where she was busy refining her eye and her taste working in fashion merchandising. An avid collector with a love of antiques, Julia quickly turned her passion for collecting into a career, first becoming an antiques dealer, then, her ultimate desire, designing dreams that have become the bold backdrops of the fashionable, the elite, and the style enthusiast.

Julia's signature vintage-modern mix (a personal favorite) is rooted in her unapologetic passion for the past, which she meticulously, unhesitatingly melds to the present, always with a great appreciation for the relevancy of how we live our lives today and beyond. Julia's unbridled ability to lavishly layer the most luxurious, contrasted with purity of form heaped with an abundance of artifacts rich in defining details, tells the story of the unabashed modern opulence that she calls Modernique".

I've always appreciated Julia's ability to throw caution to the wind with her curation of the rare, the recycled, and always the irreverent, creating interiors with fearless bravado while maintaining an underlining serenity (that speaks to a timeless sanctuary of style that is very personal to her and her clients).

With unique perspective, Julia Buckingham's style tells the tale of two cities in complete contrast to one another: She lives her life among the monolithic architectural marvels of Chicago and the picturesque arid deserts of Phoenix, Arizona. With the international experience of a world traveler, Julia Buckingham brings a global glamour and a quintessential American sensibility to each of her design projects.

Julia is also an infectious personality! And her talents are far greater than envisioning elegant environments with an edge. Julia's intuitive sensitivity celebrates the individual (instantly injecting clients' personal imprint on each and every project) and immediately transforms clients to friends, the ultimate custodians to her vivid design visions. In her unique, Modernique style, Julia Buckingham creates more than a collection of rooms: She believes wherever you hang your hat should be your ultimate home.

With the turn of each colorfully curated, artfully arranged page, *Modernique* becomes a window into a world of eclectic, eccentric elegance. Join consummate creator Julia Buckingham on her inspiring journeys to uncover the elaborately exotic and the masterfully modern: Julia Buckingham creates more than interiors, she creates an emotion, an energy, and an enlightenment to the world of Modernique.

—Ken Downing,
Senior Vice President/Fashion Director, Neiman Marcus

INTRODUCTION

Let me introduce you to the style of interior design and decoration that I call Modernique®. It blends antique with modern, and high with low. It celebrates saturated color palettes, bold patterns, and textures that say: "Touch me." It always includes flourishes of art and eccentric accessories, plus some bling and items from the world of fashion. It's not about the mix just for the sake of the mix. It's about individuality. And uniqueness. And difference. And the adventure of creating rooms and homes that are full of your own personality— and harmonious and comfortable to live in, too. If you want to feel free to trust your visual instincts, prefer surprise over predictability, and love the idea of finding and deciding what works together for you and your family rather than letting someone else tell you what's right and what matches, then Modernique is for you.

So many of us come to interior design sideways. We feel we have to follow a set of rules that define what's tasteful and what goes together. That's why finding our own style of design and decoration can be a bit stressful. We usually begin to experiment with a look when we have our first jobs and starter apartments, if we haven't already done so in our childhood bedrooms at home. Often, it'll include some hand-me-down pieces with a few new purchases. When we're ready for our next phase—moving in together—the blending of possessions occasions a whole other set of challenges. With each new stage of life, our tastes and styles continue to evolve. That process of discovery can be so much fun, and bring so much joy, especially if you're someone who leaps at the challenge of figuring out your interior aesthetic for yourself—and enjoying the way your take on it changes over time. When that's the case—as it's always been for me—you know that bucking the so-called rules of design and decoration frees you to be more creative and expressive. The more adventurous you are about taking risks and the fewer restrictions you feel you need to follow about deciding what goes with what, the more different, interesting, and distinctive your rooms become.

As a professional interior designer, I started late. It wasn't until just over a decade ago, when our youngest daughter was in middle school, that I began to design and decorate homes professionally. But I've actually been doing some form of interior design—and of Modernique—since childhood. My guess is that you have been, too. Certainly you know the way that time hones your eye. Your sensibility may well have its roots in fashion, as mine does. Even if it doesn't, you see how the two are connected through design's essential elements: form, color, pattern, texture, materials, scale, proportion, history, and details. Maybe, like me, you have always been more attracted to what's different than what matches. Perhaps you're happiest when you can collect dissimilar elements—antique, vintage, and modern—and curate, edit, and arrange them to create harmonious spaces.

My love of antiques comes from my mother, another Midwestern gal, who has always loved the forms of eighteenth-century France and England. My sensibilities, though, have always been much broader and more inclusive. When I was small, my mother and I spent a great deal of time antiquing. She would gleefully bring her finds home from those dusty old shops. Occasionally, she would trade or sell them to her friends. Two or three times a year, she and her girlfriends would open up our garage on Sheridan Road and have garage sales. Whenever she was planning her next sale, she would always ask if I had any pieces of my own that I wanted to get rid of. In retrospect, those antiquing jaunts with my mother, and her garage sales, were my interior design beginnings.

Whn I was in ninth grade, my family moved from Chicago's North Shore to Albuquerque. I was entranced by the landscape there, as well as by the mix of cultures, each with its own heritage of design and handicrafts. But for me—like for many of you, probably—fashion always came first. After graduating from the University of Arizona with a degree in fashion merchandising, I moved back to Chicago and started working at Neiman Marcus, which had recently opened its store on Michigan Avenue.

As a newlywed in Chicago, I took my first plunge into design with our first apartment. Fortunately, I had the help of my mother-in-law, an interior designer,

PAGE 4: Inspiration for pattern and palette choices can come from anywhere, including the materials of a room's interior architecture. PAGE 8: The curving, swooping shapes echo through the painting, sculpture, and chair and pull together this grouping's disparate elements. OPPOSITE: These decorative details all come from the same room and relate to one other through color and form.

MODERNIQUE 10 INTRODUCTION

who introduced me to the Merchandise Mart, among other places. My husband was completely involved with the entire process, which made creating our first home memorable and very, very fun.

Like so many city dwellers, we moved to the suburbs when we started our family—three children in five years. There, I had a "like mother, like daughter" déjà vu sort of experience (but different). With a neighbor who also enjoyed antiquing, I traveled all over the world. That led to a start-up cottage industry that involved staging rooms in a house for a weekend with all our goods—furnishings, light fixtures, rugs, art, and accessories—for sale. It grew so rapidly that we started to realize that we had a knack for putting things together.

We were just really getting going when my family moved to Cincinnati. I quickly found the town's antiquing district—and its most adorable, interesting store, located in an old Victorian house. I shopped there so much that the four ladies who ran it invited me to join them, and that's when the idea of interior design as a profession really kicked in for me. Two and a half years later, our family moved back to the North Shore and into another of the old homes of the kind my husband and I had both grown up in and have always loved. But like so many people who adore period architecture and historic houses, we wanted the interiors to fit our modern lifestyle.

When you have a passion for old houses and living with that dichotomy, and are happy to move and take on new challenges, you tend to become an eager serial renovator. That, at least, is our story. We went from an old cottage in Northbrook to a Victorian farmhouse in Wilmette to the house of my dreams in Kenilworth to, eventually, an 1876 Victorian in Wilmette, overhauling each along the way. With subsequent moves, all in all we've reinvented fifteen homes in thirty years. When it comes to architectural history, interior design, and period and contemporary styles, there's no better or more inspiring way to learn than by working hands-on with the real thing.

I had picked up the antiques business with my friend again when my family moved back from Cincinnati. People began to ask for help arranging the pieces they had

OPPOSITE: Talk about whiteouts! There must be a thousand shades of white, if not more. Combining several different variations in a range of materials, finishes, and degrees of transparency and opacity fascinates the eye. As for the vintage vase, the faces repeat all the way around the circumference—so fun!

purchased. That quickly turned into: "Can you decorate my house?" Who wouldn't leap at that opportunity? The look of course went through phases, but it always combined what in retrospect is the DNA of Modernique: antiques and unusual pieces with patina, lots of color, some bling, interesting accessories and art, and perhaps an ethnic touch or two. As Buckingham Interiors + Design LLC, I began working from home with a fax machine and a computer. In those days, what more did one need?

Just as I was beginning to outgrow my home office, an antiques-dealer friend called to tell me she had found a storefront in the West Town neighborhood of Chicago—the space where my headquarters are now. The neighborhood was funky, but on its way up. The building itself was fantastic: an old foundry, all vast open space with a vestibule and stairs. At about the same time, I became a founding contributor to Material Girls, a design blog that took off like a rocket and propelled my business to the next level. A few years later, 1stdibs came calling, which added another whole facet to my endeavors with antiques. Just recently, as my brand-licensing ventures with Global Views have started to make it to market, international business collaborations and other design-related opportunities have begun to come into focus.

Life is full of surprises. With pieces from my Global Views collection available at Neiman Marcus online, I find myself back at Neiman's once again, but differently. With design offices now in both Phoenix and Chicago, I am settled in the two places where my deepest roots lie. This allows me to continue to do what I love to do most, which is to work closely with my clients to create the residences of their dreams and to mentor the young women and men in my firm, design's next generation.

Curiosity. A taste for risk. A sense of adventure. A love of fun. A passion for fashion. An eye for what's different. An itch to mix the old with the new. These are some of the qualities that fascinate me. If they fascinate you, too, you can use them to create a home that's distinctively yours—and like no one else's. And if you do, you can continue to evolve your rooms in really interesting ways. What could be more Modernique?

OPPOSITE: In my studio and office, I constantly experiment with the idea of what transforms a group of individual pieces into a combination that's Modernique. The challenge involves finding a visual thread that brings pieces from different periods and styles into arrangements that are unusual, bold, and harmonious with a touch of humor.

MODERNIQUE

I am all for combining styles, colors, textures, materials, and periods in the same interior. How about you? If you prefer a happy mix of separates to the predictability of matching sets, that's a "yes." People like us know that difference has its own set of attractions and change offers endless opportunities for reinvention. Now take those thoughts a step or two further. Consider how much fun it can be to put together high and low, modern and antique, fine things and flea-market finds to create living spaces that are unexpectedly serene.

Balking at those rules of decorating that say rooms must come together in a certain way, and only in that way, seems to start in childhood—at least it did for me, with my matching antique bedroom set. But I didn't really start to formulate the concept of the mix until after I was married. It began within our first apartment, which my husband and I created together with the help of his mother, an interior designer. To be inventive, and budget-conscious, we went to Ace Hardware and purchased a pair of metal tool drawers—two-toned in red and black—for our living room side tables. At an estate sale across the street from my in-laws' house, we found vintage outdoor seating in black iron that we used to supplement our living room sofa. We painted the cushions black with acrylic paint and then gave them, Jackson Pollock-style, red and white splatters. The apartment, a duplex with an open plan like a loft, felt so hip to us. Because we worked on it together, the process was fun rather than anxiety-inducing. It certainly taught me two valuable lessons: that nothing needs to be expensive, and that it's possible to put together pieces with wildly different pedigrees to create an interesting and very personal look. This was just the beginning of Modernique.

We design our homes today more for family function than for elegance. We want to be able to sit in every piece of seating—in every room in the home. So bypass anything too fancy, fragile, or precious. Opt for great-looking furnishings that can withstand small children and teenagers. Let these pieces show their past lives or refresh them with a new coat of lacquer or up-to-date fabric. In my experience, when you find items that you love, they always look right together.

MIXES

STAN SHAFFER

LAYER BY LAYER

An interior develops its distinctive functionality, unique personality, and special atmosphere layer by layer—that is, through its furnishings, fabrics, finishes, light fixtures, artwork, rugs, and accessories. Every designer takes an individual approach to this layering process, to choosing and placing the elements that together make up the individual rooms. I'm not one for uniformity, predictability, or the usual flourishes and finishing touches of decoration per se.

Celebrate the different, the various, and the disparate. If you try this approach, it will free you to do the unexpected and to break what many consider unbreakable rules. Think about combining various metals with woods, crystals with patent leather, cut velvet and the patina of an antique Swedish Gustavian piece all in one room. Don't shy away from using more than one metal or metallic finish in the same item. Try mixing different textiles on individual pieces. When I'm creating a custom sofa, for example, I like to incorporate at least two distinct fabrics into its upholstery treatment—one for the exterior, another for the interior. (It's a given that these materials should be beautiful and durable. They can be high contrast, though they don't have to be.) Whether the pairing is sharply dissimilar or subtly monochromatic, the fabric that covers the sofa back, wraps the arms, and envelops the base has to attract the eye because where the eye goes, the body follows. (A design trick, by the way, that works on much more than sofas.) For me, that means materials with luscious, rich textures or with a noticeable dimensional pattern of some sort, either embossed or debossed.

What's more interesting than passing down the hallway and seeing the hind side of a beautiful sofa dressed in a fabulous fabric? We want to live on our sofas. And entertain on them. And be comfortable in them. But that doesn't mean they shouldn't be gorgeous, glamorous, and completely distinctive. That's what beauty and function together can achieve, hand in hand, layer by layer.

PAGE 17: An antique Pennsylvania Dutch farm sign becomes a piece of modern art in this Scottsdale penthouse. PRECEDING PAGES: A deep turquoise-y teal grounds the chatter of bold patterns. OPPOSITE: Even muted colors allow for infinite variations. OVERLEAF: Texture used as pattern and a palette that reflects the skyline make a comparatively small space feel much bigger.

ABOVE: The most interesting pattern in our Chicago living room comes from the heavy paint residue on an artist's work surface, repurposed as a dining table on custom lacquered pedestals. I think these lamps mimic the sleekest skyscrapers of our view. OPPOSITE: Our cerused oak cabinetry picks up on the darkest shade in the multitoned wood floor. In its own way, the acrylic cookbook stand is so like the city's glass curtain walls.

PAGES 26-27: All the objects in the fifty-sixth-floor living/dining room of this Chicago high-rise home tell a story of color, form, and personality. Teardrop shapes are one motif that repeats throughout the room. RIGHT: How do you transform a traditional room into an up-to-the-minute environment without stripping away every vestige of its history? Try a combo of groovy wallpaper set into picture moldings, slender chairs, a sofa dressed in crushed cotton velvet, and contemporary ottomans with a midcentury vibe.

In cotton velvet with a relief pattern of hand-dyed raindrops, the Miss Wiggle chair adds some curvaceous pizazz to the strict geometry of the panel moldings and introduces the color story that completely transforms the living room of this historic house on Chicago's North Shore.

White walls provide great backdrops for art, but so do those touched by color, like this fireplace wall with just the slightest tinge of blue. It brilliantly shows off Robert Robinson's startling, can't-take-your-eyes-off-it piece of graffiti art. Symmetry then works its calming magic: The flanking crystal prism sconces nod to a vintage Deco aesthetic, but are contemporary pieces of my own design.

Have you ever wondered how to place a piece of upholstery in front of a window without blocking your favorite view? A daybed can solve that particular design challenge. In contrasting upholstery fabrics, it has a definite presence and couture appeal: The crushed cotton velvet upholstery plays off the wallpaper pattern and the peacock feather design atop the ottomans, plus it adds a plush note of decadence.

NURTURED BY NATURE

If I were only allowed to offer one piece of design advice it would this: Be alert to inherent contrasts. Abstract versus representational patterns, saturated versus pale colors, bold versus subtle forms, old versus new pieces, the natural versus the man-made—these opposites just scratch the surface. When you play up the range and get the mix right for the space, it creates a truly happy energy. As long as the components align (in whichever quirky fashion), and their qualities make sense, there are no wrong choices—just clear or unexpected ones.

Leap right over predictable themes, especially with the references to nature that are so much a part of our decorative language, and steer toward creative alternatives. For example, from a fabric with a school-of-fish pattern to an oversize zinc seahorse (so much the better if it was originally a piece of a staircase railing in Palm Beach), there are so many more interesting ways than seashells to infuse an interior with notes of the life aquatic.

What makes me smile? Nature that is a little outsized, a little over the top. Gilded or lacquered ostrich eggs in a syncopated tablescape arrangement and the resin carapace of a giant tortoise displayed like a work of art. A Lucite console with an edge resembling stalactites or icicles feels chic to me. So do a bouquet of quail feathers, peacock-patterned wallpaper, a confectionary table of twigs, and ram's horn sconces that hang in perfect parentheses around a bathroom mirror.

Nature has many versions of luxury—no surprise there. But what's more crazily delicious for pillows, throws, and ottomans than a shaggy sheepskin? (When it's dyed, it's visual dynamite.) Geodes are nature's bling, and a fascinating marriage of crustiness and sparkle. A chandelier made of agate slices feels especially dreamy, like a necklace in the ceiling.

Nature nurtures our imaginations with her infinite variety. Why not use her to add drama to our rooms?

PAGE 35: A piece that's transparent adds functional glamour to most rooms. The Ice Console does that–
with a blast of cool, too. ABOVE: Walls in a deep, saturated shade create a tailored retreat for a man's home
office. OPPOSITE: To add another layer of pattern in this happily serene family room, I lined the bookshelf
interiors with wallpaper. The footstools introduce a splash of color from the breakfast room beyond.

PAGE 38: As captivatingly interesting objects go, this vintage gumball machine turned into a lamp rates pretty high. PAGE 39: For practicality and style in breakfast room seating, faux leather is a wonderful option. Then for the wow factor, just say chinoiserie! ABOVE: I love wallpaper patterns that trick the eye—like this one, of vintage postage stamps. OPPOSITE: Because space was tight, this desk had to be open. Its very graphic base gives the room a definite groove.

In my own home office in a Chicago high-rise, I work at a desk of tessellated stone—such a welcome infusion of old, Hollywood-style glamour. The multicolor hide rug adds a sense of adventure and luxury underfoot. The gleaming texture of an abstract, extravagantly imaginative work by Sarah Raskey, a favorite local artist, pulls the eye upward from the floor.

ABOVE: For life in the "bubble" behind glass-curtain walls, champagne-cork barstools at the kitchen island and a kitchen chandelier made from glass and chrome globes are perfect, stylish, and witty solutions.
OPPOSITE: This apartment's magnificent view of Lake Michigan inspired the custom water-patterned wallpaper. With the look of an underwater creature, a vintage Brutalist mirror feels right at home.

Bling doesn't have to mean flash, facets, and sparkles. In a room of quietly luxurious neutrals, it can be as subtle as the blown-up quartz chips by Brenda Houston that cover the wall behind the bed or as lustrous as the gilding on the birch bedposts and the saguaro sculpture atop the midcentury bedside table.

ABOVE: In this bath, the mirrors introduce unexpected notes of color and the floor tiles read like sea glass. OPPOSITE: This young equestrienne's bedroom is all about texture, texture, and more texture. But since she's not into high visual drama, the dimensional levels are subdued. What enhances the overall effect is their interplay, like that between the gilded feather-covered pillows and the shagreen headboard.

PATTERN

Pattern and texture send me over the moon. They are the elements of design that make a room most dynamic (along with color). I see them as twins, or at least flip sides of the same decorative coin. Here's why: Pattern creates visual texture and texture creates visual pattern. So, whether they're performing solo or as a duet, pattern and texture tickle our senses of sight and touch. Because their effect is multidimensional and cumulative, they heighten our perceptions of and our responses to the spaces we inhabit.

Some people are innately pattern people. Others I do my best to convert. Why? Simple or complex geometrics, swoon-inducing ombrés, full-on florals, sassy animal prints—every single one of them creates options for all kinds of décor fun.

In design terms, pattern wakes up a room. It may do so with loud bravado and unabashed charm, or with a gentle, understated whisper. For me, the joy—and the art— of working with pattern comes from selecting and editing, coupling this pattern with that, finding the right complementary palette, and then pairing that combination with however many others. That's really my state of play. Factor in the possibilities that three-dimensional wall coverings or textiles can add. Imagine what's possible by layering textures on fabrics and furniture. Just going bold with a pattern on a well-shaped chair can bring a cheering bit of whimsy to a room—or electrify it with pizazz.

With pattern, there are no real, hard rules. It may feel almost instinctive to go for the unembellished and unadorned. Patternless mohairs, cotton velvets, linens, and silks are always beautiful, elegant, and easy on the eyes. And I am fine with them as far as they go. But if you're someone who habitually prefers solids, it may be time to take a leap and embrace the risk. Dip a toe (or more) into pattern's kaleidoscopic world, and there will be no more cold feet. You can find your inner taste for leopard—or stripes, swirls, links, polka dots, concentric circles, you name it. Once that happens, you will probably change your spots. That's the power of pattern, and its best gift of all.

PLAY

PAGE 51: The strong colors of this patterned wallpaper (yes, the birds are overscale) read more quietly than you might expect because of the way they engage with one another and with the elements and materials close by. RIGHT: For a traditionally detailed house in a bucolic landscape, a dining room done in bold, all-over pattern with sleek modern furnishings feels unexpectedly urban and sophisticated. That suits the client to a tee, yet it speaks to the context, too.

ABOVE: A custom-designed hall table at the foot of a gracefully curved stair wakes up a large, predictable central foyer by adding energy and texture through its facets and reflections. OPPOSITE: Pattern, pattern on the wall, which adds the most pizazz of them all? Dimensional wall tiles (and moldings painted to match) turn an everyday stair into a quiet theatrical feat. The light fixture adds the crowning twist.

PRECEDING PAGES: For anyone enamored with bold color and pattern, this living room says it all. The sofa with its happy cushions beckons all comers, an inviting presence at the room's far end. ABOVE: This chandelier is a true piece of jewelry–and beyond alluring when lit. OPPOSITE: On a mirrored coffee table, interesting objects create layer after layer of fascinating reflections.

When I'm designing interiors for a historic home, I always ask myself this: What can I save from the past and still make the rooms current? This house, for example, still has its very beautiful leaded glass windows and original moldings. To bring the living room up to date, we chose furnishings that span the divide: Chairs with hints of traditional forms, a comfy but elegant contemporary sofa, bold coffee table, sleek étagère, and modern art. The rug's strong pattern pulls the whole mix together.

OPPOSITE: This house had a huge entry hall that felt like a chilly greeting. To take advantage of the unused space in a way that was welcoming and functional, we turned part of it into a seating area. ABOVE: We did something similar with the front hall bay, which is now where the children of the house do their homework. The patterned wallpaper ties the two areas together and helps to bring the vintage elements up to date.

ABOVE: With its gutsy furniture, a mysterious painting, and look-at-me wallpaper, this room is perfectly modern. For some unconventional DIY holiday bling: We spray painted branches silver and draped them with matching ornaments. OPPOSITE: Sometimes the only place for the bed is in front of a window—yikes—yet draping the entire wall behind the bed helps suggest a serene sleeping nook.

This room used to be monochromatic and somehow it never felt special, even with those fabulous windows. Now it contains multiple layers of strong patterns in an interesting palette, and it couldn't be more alive. One unexpected benefit of this unexpected transformation? The oversize lantern, a holdover from the home's prior owners, now looks like it was made for the room.

ABOVE: Subtle, understated materials—like wallpaper with tiny glass beads or a mother-of-pearl door panel—can create truly memorable effects. OPPOSITE: For me, everyday objects are full-throttle muses for experimentation. When you reinvent your favorite things by using them in uncommon ways ("Who plants in a vintage Murano glass vessel?" *Why not?*), they can and do become extraordinary.

THEMES
AND VARIATIONS

Difference attracts me. If I had to describe this design approach as a recipe, the ingredients would be an odd lot: a high-low mix of antique, vintage, and contemporary furnishings, art, and objects. While I am clearly not one to choose a direct match over a less-obvious mate, the goal is always to establish an energized visual harmony. The individual pieces may seem a bit eccentric, because for me that's essential to their charm. Once everything's in place, though, the whole comes together in ways that make very good design sense.

Like anyone decorating a room, I give my choices plenty of thought, yet they're also deeply instinctive. Once a space is finished, I inevitably discover visual motifs, themes, or threads of form, color, pattern, scale, or materials that pull everything into a happy, serene, practical whole.

I'm not always hyperconscious of the themes-and-variations dynamic—but it is possible, and good practice, too (especially at the start of a project), to focus on it and train your eye to see things as a play on repetition.

My Phoenix living room, for example, has walls and floors made of pieces of petrified wood linked together by mortar—so midcentury modern! In this room I've included a gilded, very curvaceous bergère with its seat and back covered in an Hermès textile featuring oversize links. There's a table made from a ship's anchor with a chain. On top of that table sits a wooden tray with gilded edges with chain-link pattern on its interior. Another chair has a quasi-chain pattern inlaid in metal. There's also a tall, skinny, hide-covered chair; the spots on that hide resemble, yes, you guessed it. I know I wasn't thinking "links" when I put the room together. The architectural finishes set the stage for the interplay of distinct elements. It's repetition with a difference. And that's the idea behind themes and variations.

Risk takers who said they wanted to live in a space that puts the exclamation mark in "Wow!", these homeowners went for it with every single design decision and all the countless details. To keep the visual adventures in balance, enter the calming power of symmetry. Another coordinating feature of their rooms: The divergent forms and graphic motifs relate to one another through complementary geometries.

ABOVE: A custom sofa should look like what it is: made just for you. In my opinion, that means it should include at least two different fabrics. Or, like this one, five! OPPOSITE, CLOCKWISE FROM TOP LEFT: Polished brass spheres, cut velvet curtains, decorative white quartz studs, an exposed wood frame showing its patina and inset with several textiles–every detail in this room contributes to a harmonious take on texture.

RIGHT: Luxurious fabrics with subtle, meaningful patterns energize this monochromatic look, which suits the more traditional sensibility of these homeowners. PAGE 76: In the dining room, a paneled wainscot sets the stage for an Arts and Crafts meets Art Deco ambience. The wallpaper pattern suits the architecture and provides an interesting background for the art, which includes a beautiful contemporary diptych. PAGE 77: An artwork made with layers of wax adds an ethereal note, while the midcentury lamp offers a welcome jolt with colors completely in sync with one another.

ABOVE: Snakeskin's complicated patterns and tone-on-tone shadings work like a charm–mesmerizing.
OPPOSITE: Here snakeskin brings its powers of enhancement to everything that surrounds it:
a neutral color palette, understated textures, and rich, dark woods. Accents of hot colors add just
the right rays of sunniness and warmth to elevate this quiet, sophisticated, light-filled space.

ABOVE: I believe we should live in every part of our homes, so I do my best to make every inch functional and fun. A nook like this one offers just the perfect spot for a game table and contemporary wing chairs. OPPOSITE, CLOCKWISE FROM TOP LEFT: The details in this home clearly speak of a preference for clean geometries, quiet patterns, traditionally inspired forms, and soft tones in luxurious materials.

ABOVE: Every space offers a new opportunity for design. In a beverage center off the butler's pantry (conveniently located between the kitchen and the family area), layers of finishes and textures marry the honed with the hammered, polished, glazed, and woven. OPPOSITE: Deliberately mismatched stools add notes of whimsy to a very large traditional kitchen.

OPPOSITE: A home's existing architectural detail and ornamentation can be incredibly inspiring; here, it provided design cues for every room. ABOVE: Every object, pattern, texture, color, form—you name it—has its own distinctive personality, but can change character depending on what you put it with and how you use it. That morphing experience is part of what makes design so interesting, challenging, and fun.

PRECEDING PAGES: As themes and variations go, fretwork motifs offer incredibly rich possibilities. Different versions of the go-to pattern work their way through this family room. In the large traditional kitchen, a troika of beaded chandeliers introduces an unexpected textural twist. RIGHT: This kitchen is a recipe for layering color, pattern, and texture. The island's countertop is highly polished petrified wood—a mind-bending combo with the Missoni-style custom tiles.

ABOVE: The breakfast nook's antique Hungarian table was perfect, except it was too low.
To solve that problem, I created a base that raised it to standard dining height (30 inches).
OPPOSITE, CLOCKWISE FROM TOP LEFT: The zigzag motif goes out of doors; an upholstered
window seat overlooks the view; for these made-to-order tiles, custom meant hand-selecting
each color and proportion of colors; vintage barware takes color cues from the countertop.

ABOVE: This crazy wallpaper gives dimension to a long narrow hallway and frames the view so intriguingly.
OPPOSITE: Luxurious in its largeness, this bath still longed for an aura of intimacy. Subtly patterned wallpaper, understated window treatment fabrics, a plush shag rug, cushy linens, and figured marble accomplish that. The smaller scale of the furnishings and light fixture really draw the eye to the varied details.

ABOVE: A powder room is one place in the home where you can let your imagination run free. The vanity here, a repurposed antique kitchen cabinet that's a holdover from the home's previous owner, was a given. Among the luxe materials, patterns, and textures, it takes on a contemporary vibe. OPPOSITE: Natural wood veneers with bling? It may not be the most obvious pairing, especially with antiques and acrylic, but—shazam!

GRAPHIC

Nothing contributes more to achieving rooms with va-va-voom than some form of pure graphic glamour. Eye-catching shapes, mesmerizing lines, captivating patterns that we can't look away from, objects that tell a story in a way that demands our attention—these are the kinds of graphic elements that I love to layer into my interiors. When a graphic device has the kind of indefinable oomph that makes it feel just right as a room's focal point—a custom white wall-unit with compartments outlined boldly in black, or a tracery of mullions over mirrored dressing-room doors, just for example—that's when you can use it as a building block for the rest of the room's design.

The sparks for these graphic elements always fly from the personality of the homeowner, I find. For someone who loves rhinestones and crystal embellishments, I might envision bling-filled rooms based on the idea of facets and angles. If stars are the fascination, the star shape might become the DNA of my design.

There are so many elements of design that you can use to establish or enhance your graphic theme. Wallpaper is always a great go-to because it can convey the language of pattern in a truly powerful, even mesmerizing way. This is true whether you use that wallpaper for the entire room, for a feature wall, or for a fun accent on a dado, wainscot, or ceiling.

Art and accessories can drive home the visual drama, and tell a story, too. Early in my career, I had a formative experience in using art and accessories for both purposes. I was working on an office for a graphic designer, a very talented, creative friend of my husband's. I had found a group of super-cool antique pieces—a giant quill pen, a gigantic paintbrush, a ginormous pencil—all crafted originally as shop signs and professional signifiers. They were off-the-charts quirky. They expressed his passions. And they represented the tools of his trade and his art in the most graphic terms possible. Once they were hung, they reminded him of the long tradition of his professional art—and told his clients something special about him.

The catalyst for graphic magic can be almost anything. What's key is that it strikes a deep, positive emotional chord. So trust your wildest design impulses when they're setting off the alarm bells, because your instincts never lie.

GLAMOUR

PAGE 97: Hello, blingville! Here's to sparkle—the more, the merrier. The facets and spikes that brighten this foyer echo through a fabulous Fornasetti wall covering designed specifically for chair rails. ABOVE AND OPPOSITE: These two sides of an entry hall face each other. The base of the Tangle table chats intimately with the stair rail, while a jewel-encrusted artwork by Sarah Raskey comments on the sideboard doors below.

When the architectural framework of an interior is as essential, elegant, and expressive as it is here, rejoice and go with it. The proportions, profiles, and geometries of these molding details present a perfect springboard for design interpretation. That's why each piece of furniture in this room—and all the lighting, accessories, and artwork—emphasizes the sculptural and textural over the purely decorative and ornamental.

OPPOSITE: To those who say, "Don't mix metals," I say, "Au contraire!" Metals are their own distinctive palette of colors and textures, and I love working with them in that way. As they swoop, swirl, and corner their way through this room, they add focus and delicate definition to the room's various dimensions. ABOVE: What's more surprising then shelving units with such unexpected storage/display spaces for books and artifacts?

ABOVE: Gold on gold—it's so very magical in all kinds of light! OPPOSITE: Dining rooms should be special day and night. They're everyday rooms with a designated and distinctive purpose, and they're spaces we want to make memorable through the drama and fantasy of design. Here, a combination of metal finishes infuses more than a bit of both into this architecturally elegant space, which is otherwise rather restrained.

ABOVE: This room's pièce de résistance is clearly the chandelier. A one-of-a-kind fixture by Louise Gaskill, it incorporates some amazing vintage finds, like the finial elements and a fab Murano glass ball.
OPPOSITE: Walls covered in silver-leafed grass cloth make this room shimmer subtly at all hours and provide such a cool backdrop for antique building ornaments. The midcentury sideboard is a prized family possession.

The palette of this luminous jewel box
of a sitting room speaks to the natural
wonder that is Lake Michigan beyond
(with its fifty shades or more of gray).
The sinuous lines of the chaises wind
their way through the room in so many
different guises, materials, and scales.
And, really, what could be a more
brazen—or glam—finishing touch than a
crystal-studded black leather chandelier?

BRINGING THE BLING

Every woman wants some sort of feminine touch in her environment—and not just in the master bedroom, the master bath, or her dressing room. My accessories of choice for this purpose are chandeliers. I always treat them as the interior design equivalent of jewelry, so I choose and place them to add the final ornamental flourish that every room (like every outfit) deserves.

For inherent glamour, nothing beats a touch of sparkle, especially when your taste tends that way. But there's more design value to bling than you might think, especially if bling is not your thing. You can use a shiny, reflective surface or two (or more!) to capture the light and make it dance through space. And since nothing draws the eye faster than sheen and sparkle, you can place those elements just so to direct the eye exactly where you'd like it to go. A sequined pillow, a mirrored coffee table, a metallic furniture finish, a reflective fireplace surround, a hammered metal bowl, beaded and bejeweled candlesticks—sure, they're fun. But they're far more than that should you want them to be.

Fashion fiend that I am, I also love to incorporate items from the world of fashion—and actual pieces of jewelry—as accessories. I do this in my own rooms, and in many of my clients'. Why not drape necklaces and other trinkets across tabletop vignettes? Or create a centerpiece with beads, baubles, and trinkets instead of cut flowers? Or set brooches and rings here and there on shelving units and in display cases to scatter that extra bit of stardust that glitter in moderation can provide. When you do, you'll find that these everyday ornaments serve almost like spotlights as they highlight what they're adorning.

OPPOSITE: A gorgeously set table always incorporates materials that bring the bling. OVERLEAF: To do a room that's simply white—that's a trial in restraint. That there are at least a thousand shades of white makes things interesting. Fold in the hues that are just off white and the combinations start to boggle. Then factor in the way white reveals itself in different materials, textures, and finishes, and snap: It's a fantasia.

CAPTIVATING CHANDELIERS

In lighting, my rule of thumb is that bigger is always better. A chandelier—or any overhead fixture with a commanding presence—offers the perfect opportunity to stretch the predictable comfort zone for scale and proportion.

When we walk into a space most of us look up first, not down, so we immediately notice any hanging elements of décor. However beautiful the furnishings and palette may be, a piece of jewelry center stage—one that gives cause for pausing and gasping because it's so unique—provides far more than a visual exclamation point. It creates an organizing principle at the room's core.

No matter where you are, keep an eye out for unusual, original contemporary fixtures and exceptional vintage lighting. Or work with your designer to commission one-of-a-kind pieces from your favorite craftspeople. For materials and colors, there really are no rules. Glass? Obviously. Metals? Yes, but why not be daring with them also? Old-school standards of style say that metals need to match. I say, mix them—the more, the better! Rose gold. Brass. Polished nickel. Chrome. Pewter. Silver. You name it. I find that they can work together because, remember, they are all related.

If the search for a unique fixture comes up empty and commissioning one from an artisan isn't an option, it's time to flex the creativity and think differently. A cluster of individual pendants, for example, can serve the purpose beautifully. Arrange the elements according to proportion, color, and style on cords of different lengths. By design, it's an expressive centerpiece that's full of personality.

There's something wonderful about an unexpected element of lighting that may not put function first. A kiwi branch sculpture with just one bulb has been hanging in my office forever. It's showing a bit of wear because I've moved it around so often, but it still looks fantastic. Be adventurous. If you love a light fixture that drips feathers, or that looks like a cumulus cloud, or that resembles a cascade of falling icicles, or even a groovy tumbleweed (as is the case with one of my favorite clients), go for it—and make it your own.

OPPOSITE: In a stairwell as high as this (three stories), one hanging fixture would have been cute. But don't you think a towering space really calls for more? Since I couldn't find a chandelier that did the trick, I decided to make one—with fifteen pendants, attached to one canopy, cascading to different heights—a unique solution that gives this unusual volume its due.

ABOVE: A delicate wire sphere filled to bursting with shiny glass orbs—what could be more simple, or more complicated, or more jewel-like? OPPOSITE: Eye-catching as it is, this chandelier works to quiet a room that shimmies with leather fringe, lots of reflective surfaces, and a mesmerizing artwork by Richard Shipps. The lion's heads? They're architectural fragments, and they mean so much to the homeowner, a Leo.

OPPOSITE: This frothy, bubble-icious light fixture plays off the ceiling tracery and the colored blobs that swirl their way across the canvas behind it. ABOVE: It also picks up on the texture and pattern of the sideboard doors and nods (in its modern way) to the grape clusters grasped by the putti that adorn the cast antique mirror frame—such happy pairings, made through so many distinctive contrasts.

OPPOSITE: In an understated, softly textured room full of pale neutrals, the artwork does the heavy lifting with color. The subtlest glints of metal and reflection at various levels from floor to ceiling give so much definition and focus to a room. ABOVE: This chandelier is my own design. I call it Jewel Tangle, and it incorporates a midcentury piece at its heart.

OPPOSITE: A redone kitchen helps to bring the idea of outdoor living inside, transforming the home of transplanted Bostonians (inspired by northern California) who love to cook. The quartet of photographs could easily be discussing design dialectics with the horn chandelier. And, of course, the combo adds a graphic pop. ABOVE: In the adjacent dining area, multiple glass pendants energize the space overhead.

ABOVE: This delicate lovely holds all the keys to my heart! OPPOSITE: A casual family dining area tells another story of spatial creativity: It transforms a formerly unused corner adjacent to the back door. The seat backs are low enough not to block the view. Vintage cutting boards, collected over the years, hang in a prominent spot. They add a touch of tongue-in-cheek charm, and feel totally appropriate.

ABOVE: Custom-made pocket doors that enclose the breakfast room from the dining room are very useful for privacy but allow for light to pass between the two spaces. OPPOSITE: Curves, spheres, squaring the circle—all these motifs relate to one another in the mix of furnishings, objects, and details. They're like a defined but delicate tracery that pulls together an airy, understated, seriously elegant dining room.

LEFT: From the gold-finished cages of the light fixtures to the nickel inserts in the stonework behind the oven, the metallic gleams provide some visual spice that jazzes up this spacious kitchen in an understated way. ABOVE: This little treasure of a decorative bowl does double duty for storage and display.

With a spectacular view that extends this bath practically into Lake Michigan, this master retreat is one home spa space that you could properly call a natatorium! Adding to the feeling of intimacy here, I decided to make the elements of this room do "the wave." The swoops and curves mimic one another and undulate from one piece to the next, including the custom vanity that stretches along a twenty-two-foot wall.

130

OPPOSITE: With its tone-on-tone exploration of finishes from matte to metal and its use of ultra luxurious fabrics and materials, this silvery master bedroom looks and feels completely dreamy.
ABOVE: The story of this dressing room is about finding inspiration in pattern, and then using it in every element of the room to elevate the entire design. The chandelier makes its own contribution.

PRECEDING PAGES: An exercise in opulence, this bedroom incorporates lavish materials and sumptuous details from floor to ceiling. ABOVE: Okay, ombré! This unusual tile mosaic adds color, texture, and glamour to the bath. The white mosaic tile starts on the ceiling (mimicking the shape of the tub) then gets darker as it goes down the wall and darker still as it wraps the tub toward the base. OPPOSITE: This bathroom tells a tale of reflections as light pings back and forth between the mirrored surfaces and off the custom vanity's iridescent shell tiles.

FASHION

If you're fashion-obsessed like me, you've been training your eye since an early age to see and assess what looks right, trendy, funky, fabulous, inspired, chic, new, and above all, you—item by item, outfit by outfit. Those ideas translate from fashion to interior design, and back again.

Fashion and interior design both involve a unique blending of so many of the same factors. Each is definitely its own form of alchemy, but they are also cross-pollinators from way back. At any given time in any given era, we could probably trace the way the shape of a heel influences the form of a chair's foot, or vice versa; how the particular cut and padding of a garment's shoulder inspires the sinuous form of a sofa back or arm; how a layering of cashmere over voile might translate into a window treatment. Season by season, decade by decade, color trends in one field flow into the other's most popular palettes. The same is true for patterns, textures, and materials, and even for ideas about what makes the eye happy in terms of proportion and scale.

So how can you bring a fashion sensibility to your interiors? One immediate way is by incorporating apparel fabrics into your design scheme as pillow coverings or at the window, for upholstery, or to dress a bed or a table. You can also have interior design fun with fashion's ornaments, like studs, grommets, fringes, and all sorts of other embellishments, whether classic or of the moment. Then there are the dressmaker details. Like a well-placed gusset or an architected dart on a favorite piece of clothing, a sharp box pleat or a voluptuous ruffle (just for starters) can add nuance and a made-to-fit-for-the-occasion quality to a piece of upholstery. From an accessories point of view, fashion elements like vintage hat or shoe forms, or a plaster bust with a jeweled necklace draped into its décolletage, can also speak volumes about personal style.

Many people have waxed eloquent about the language of apparel, the meaning of fashion, and how the worlds of fashion and interior design relate to each other. What it comes down to is this: Whether we're dressing our homes for our everyday lifestyle or our selves for the day, the same judgment, sensibility, and curatorial eye are always at work.

STATEMENTS

PAGE 139: On our upstairs landing, fashion references play happily with antiques and organic elements. A massive gilded frame gives this contemporary canvas greater significance. OPPOSITE: The front hall of our 1876 Victorian lacked a closet, so we converted a Louis Philippe armoire, a family heirloom. ABOVE: The giant zinc greeter is a piece of architectural salvage recovered from a building facade in New York City.

OPPOSITE: Because the entry had no overhead fixture and it was problematic to rewire for one, we added electrified antique lanterns atop the newel posts for illumination. A caribou pelt (a hairy monster) drapes over a midcentury leather bench for texture in a front hall nook. ABOVE: The wonderful artist Maggie Meiners created the silhouettes of our children; the colors play off the leaded glass windows.

OPPOSITE: Our living room has a wabi-sabi sort of feel. It's my homage to the idea of the imperfectly perfect. The pieces are all about comfort (and fashion). Our dogs love to hang on the turquoise sofa and watch the world go by. They also take ownership of our leather and hide lounge chair. ABOVE: Our coffee table is an antique pallet on wheels. A vintage nut dispenser is a perfect display case for the arrangements of objects that I change regularly, which I do according to my latest fashion craze.

ABOVE: With my last name, what better to collect than crowns? I am always on the lookout for another antique, vintage, or contemporary version to add to my royal treasures. They come in an endless array of shapes, sizes, and metals, which makes them so intriguing and fun to display. OPPOSITE: Suited in one of Paul Smith's signature stripes, a modern sofa feels right at home in a Victorian living room.

Each piece here has great personal meaning. Elvira, the bejeweled bust, has been in my husband's family for years. The fanciful Julie Blackmon photograph features three children, like ours. The French chandelier comes from one of our previous homes; we had found it there, reconstructed it, and couldn't leave it behind. Antique portraits—our pseudo family—add their own personalities. The built-in breakfront that serves as a cabinet for curiosities is original to the house, and a keeper.

MADE BY HAND

When you find something unique and beautiful—especially when it is something incredible that has been made by hand—that is a eureka moment. Artisan-made items add such personality and emotional texture to their environments. A one-of-a-kind element commissioned for a particular spot in a home helps make that home original. Plus the collaborative creative process when it goes well is more fun than just about anything else in design.

One of my favorite artists, Gian Garofalo, makes these vibrant, modern, drip-painted wood pieces that have a rough-hewn quality. To create his palette, he mixes pigments with a clear epoxy resin. Then he painstakingly applies the different hues, stripe by stripe, coat upon coat, letting gravity work its magic. At the bottom of each of his pieces, the epoxy dries into these marvelous drips of different lengths and thicknesses. The color sings. The textures are fantastic. The effect feels totally organic.

Anna Wolfson is one of the Chicago-area artisans I feel privileged to work with on any project. She puts the handmade into a space in a really unusual way, by coating walls in burlap (sourced from my favorite family-owned fabric houses) that she feathers and fringes by hand and finishes with color. I always think of her up on the scaffold, transforming whatever room she's working in with her art and her craft.

I also love the idea of repurposing as a form of artisanship. I occasionally work with Julie Harris, who collects vintage bathing suits. After selecting and grouping the individual suits, she then frames them museum-style. I might hang one solo on a wall—or cover a wall with them gallery-style. To say those suits from the fifties or sixties are amazing is an understatement, and when they're hung massed together they're completely unexpected as wallpaper. So whether you find a work of art that you love, commission a piece or a special effect just because, or work with someone to repurpose existing items in an artful way, the handcrafted, artisan-made elements of your home will put you totally in the swim of things decoratively speaking.

OPPOSITE: Gian Garofalo's brilliantly colored drip painting has such incredible texture and pattern. I love the intricate process he uses to make his pieces. I love even more the contrast between its sleek-yet-textured surface and the distressed materials that it hangs above, the points of the crowns that reach up to meet its drips, and the play of the circular geometries both horizontal and vertical.

RIGHT: The parlor contains so many fashion references, both high and low. First, there's the divine Audrey Hepburn: This midcentury poster of her—an ad for a raincoat company—is by the illustrator René Gruau. Cathy Daley's oil pastel on vellum on the other side of the window bay is such a great comment on women in motion. As for the pouf, it's made from recycled flip-flops. PAGES 154-155: Details from the living and dining rooms show how the Swedish Gustavian aesthetic fits organically into a Victorian home, especially when it's juxtaposed with surprising, eccentric, and modern pieces.

ABOVE: Jane, one of our Wheaten Terriers, has her spot by the kitchen door. The Fornasetti wallpaper has a vintage appeal that feels just right in our Victorian farmhouse. OPPOSITE: When we renovated the kitchen, we kept the original floor. Painting the maple floorboards helped to lighten up the room.

ABOVE: Carving a master bedroom suite out of the third-floor attic created some fantastically interesting rooms and various nooks and crannies. The house had a turret, so in its third-floor space we installed a cozy reading room with our children's outgrown beanbag furniture and newly built-in shelves and banquettes. OPPOSITE: One of the top-of-the-house spaces proved to be the perfect spot for Le Corbusier's modern classic.

DRESSMAKER DETAILS

Furniture pieces, lighting, objects, and art all have their own personalities. Yes, they're a room's inanimate inhabitants. But they're much more than that as well. They seem to talk to one another—and to us—through the language of design. Through their essential elements and especially through their details they can make us feel so many different emotions.

Some forms feel inherently feminine—others, decidedly masculine. The personality of each piece emerges through a combination of form, function, materials, color, and finishing touches. That's why dressmaker details are so important—and so fun. A welt or pleat can transform a taciturn-looking sofa into a confident, elegant-looking one, while a ruffle or a flounce always brings out the charm. Fringe is another option. Since it comes in myriad lengths and styles, it has more personas than anyone can count. Recently I had a dressmaker in New York City attach long, leather fringe to a pair of classic swivel chairs—talk about putting the flirt on!

The finishing flourishes needn't speak loudly. They can be quiet and nuanced and just as effective. Think about that pair of matching lounge chairs that so often face the living room sofa. How much more interesting would they be if they were dressed in similar, but not identical fabrics? Why not differentiate the partners in the pair with dressmaker details? What if one also had a button-tufted back while the other were left plain? Sure, there's a risk in doing something so unexpected. But designing with dressmaker details like these can create a pairing where each partner enhances the other through complementary personal styles. That sounds to me like a well-matched couple—and a very well-dressed one.

OPPOSITE: I may have been in my country Swedish phase when I designed our master bedroom, but I still had to mix in pieces from other eras and styles. A cotton velvet headboard—so plush and comfortable! The pillow materials—an antique rug, linen, and a supersize rope-cord trim—enhance the textural contrast. A fantastic faceted acrylic fixture introduces a groovy sensibility overhead.

OPPOSITE: The mix includes an antique English dress form next to a British colonial captain's cabinet filled with favorite treasures. ABOVE: Light filters through the rafters. OVERLEAF: In another nook, this sitting area centers on a Swedish Gustavian daybed and deliberately mismatched pair of side tables—one of cactus spines, the other, acrylic.

LEFT: Presiding over the dressing room is Tom Dixon's iconic copper pendant. The twig table base is a great piece of folk art that brings an organic element into our aerie in the trees. ABOVE: One of my beloved grandmother's leather-covered childhood books keeps her memory always near and dear.

OPPOSITE: This tiny powder room under the stairs was probably made by converting a closet. Old silver rose jars—all topsy-turvy—surround a wire sculpture. ABOVE: The antique mirror? It's tiny, but it fits this room perfectly.

Our oldest daughter's room was probably the
original master bedroom. Flanking her bed, set
cozily into the window bay, are self-portraits.

OPPOSITE, CLOCKWISE FROM TOP LEFT: I set a mirror in the corner of this bath intending to hang it later, but when it seemed so at home, I decided to leave it there; a rock-crystal chandelier introduces a delicate sense of wonder and a modern spirit; sconces add to the magical effect; a collection of vintage game pieces parade on the windowsill. ABOVE: Both the ceiling and the claw-foot tub are original to the house.

BOLD

If you're like me, you're always on the hunt for eye-catching pieces, patterns, palettes, accessories, and captivating mixes that feel fresh, unusual, and interesting. These are the bold gestures of design, and they start with the items of décor that really suit your personality to a tee. If you're adventurous, you can use these furnishings, fabrics, objects, and art to infuse your home with your personal character. Putting a room and home together this way takes confidence. But when you're a cockeyed optimist with a taste for risk and a love of whimsy, going bold will feel, well, just like coming home. Of course, with each room, you must first fearlessly ask yourself: "What's the craziest, coolest thing I can do?" And whatever the answer, don't be afraid to push the envelope.

The most daring design choices are always deeply instinctive, but there's a kind of logic behind them, too. That's because our emotions never lie. We love what we love what we love, even if we're not always able to analyze quite why. That's as true for the colors, forms, materials, proportions, textures, and interior design styles that make our hearts sing when we see them as it is for everything else in life.

The terrific secret of bold rooms is this: Elements and furnishings that shouldn't work together actually do. Consider this brave mix, just as an example. Imagine two slim, high-backed midcentury chairs in patterned teal velvet flanking a turquoise velvet, nailhead-trimmed, transitional sofa, all facing a faceted coffee table. Squaring the seating circle? Taborets, upholstered in a peacock print, with wavy, gold-wire bases. Then picture the entire combo within a living room graciously outlined with traditional moldings. The kicker? Shiburi-style wallpaper set into the room's picture panels. On paper, you think: "No way!" But, surprise—the various blues provide one unifying thread, and the blobular shapes, another. There may not be a definitive intellectual reason for why these combinations work so well, but there's a very definite visual rhyme. You'll know when it's developing and when it's right because—like me—you'll see it in your mind's eye.

Nothing feels better than finding an audacious, functional choice that suits the space and that sparks a smile, too. That is the biggest thrill of all.

GESTURES

PAGE 175: The original owner of this Arizona house collected the petrified wood fragments that his architect incorporated into walls and floor. Every other element of the living room plays off the structural materials. LEFT: For a homeowner who loves color, wit, and crazy, bold pieces, this Michigan Avenue apartment really goes to town. OVERLEAF: Quirky, interesting, look-at-me designs provide a strong contrast to the mesmerizing views. The living room coffee table incorporates salvaged playground equipment; the mirror frame, repurposed ceiling tiles; and an art piece, framed carnival barkers' hats.

In a convenient kitchen nook, an inviting circular sofa in a brash print allows for relaxing, chatting, and taking in the various views, exterior and interior.

This dining-room table has a well-kept secret: The top lifts off to reveal a billiards table. To balance the power of the view, Fornasetti panels (survivors from a three-panel screen) make a can't-miss statement. The chairs are also unexpected: Originally intended for exterior use, here, in cotton velvet, they've got their indoor outfits on.

SCALE IT UP, SCALE IT DOWN

In interior design and decoration, as in life, there are no second chances when it comes to first impressions. So, start every project by thinking long and hard about how to catch and hold the eye of the person crossing the threshold. Shiny, sparkly, or colorful objects, for example, serve as natural attractors. They're essential visual magnets, and important to the Modernique aesthetic. Playing with scale—mixing, matching, and calibrating the various dimensions and proportions—is another form of visual g-force. And it's a doozy.

Size matters in design, in every way. When larger-than-life meets everyday-size it creates a fantastic combination, the kind of conversation among forms that occurs when two tall pieces and one tiny piece interact as part of a vignette. Is there an "Alice in Wonderland" quality about relationships such as these? Yes. Risk, reward, adventure: that's what "Try me" is all about. Don't be afraid to pair large with small—or gargantuan with teensy. Think about breaking away from arrangements that put small with medium and large, the pleasing but predictable graduation in sizes.

Mastery of scale depends on finding a kind of internal logic for variety through height, diameter, and proportion. That way, it's possible to achieve the greatest visual impact within the given parameters of the design challenge. Whether it's a vignette, a tablescape, a seating arrangement, or an entire room, difference—not sameness—is what captivates the eye.

OPPOSITE: A proper game table shows its poker face here. The roundel of the chair back is blackboard, which is such a fun option for creating place cards (or other messages). A supersize, antique wooden blade—once a sign for a knife shop—artfully slices the space over a midcentury console. Unearthed mercury glass bottles pick up on the table's gleam theme.

Context is so important in the decision-making process. Sometimes it feels right that the elements of a room blend with the outdoors. Sometimes, a room craves high contrast. In this Scottsdale kitchen, black maple cabinets diverge from the exterior's desert tones to set a glamorous scene. Brass highlights twinkle in the tilework behind the stove and also pick up on the island base's gold-leafed carved millwork.

ABOVE: On the counter of the kitchen island, all the accessories carry on the conversation started by the kitchen's color palette and textural motifs. OPPOSITE: Why do the usual thing with hardware in a space that's all about high drama? With such amazing options now for pulls and handles, why not use them to bejewel a room that calls for those little notes of extra shine?

The world within these
windows reflects the
sweeping spaces and vistas
of high-rise living. A serene
palette of neutrals borrows its
tonalities from the view and
helps to show off a fabulous
art collection. Layers of
texture add dashes of intrigue
to the tonal harmonies.

ABOVE: With a view as spectacular as this, who wants to compete? But the home remains expressive in its furnishings, fabrics, and finishes; all have distinct, if understated, personalities. OPPOSITE: Thanks to a custom daybed, this room does double duty for visiting children or guests. The chandelier is made from repurposed vintage industrial glass reinforced with chicken wire.

The dividing line of this room's chair rail was so provocative that it called out for a two-toned wall. That in turn sparked another possibility. Two colors, done in different but equally "touch-me" textures: a deeply embossed Lincrusta (on the lower half), and a heavily distressed faux leather (on the upper).

ABOVE: Tony Duquette's voluptuous table takes—and holds—center stage. OPPOSITE: Each curio and collectible introduces another tonal twist to the textural drama. Whitewashed seedpods and alabaster grapes nest inside glass canisters. Parchment-bound books provide subtle definition and a kind of architecture framed by two Asian ceramics. Contemporary ceramics with a rough, organic, grass-inspired finish fold another organic quality into the mix.

As bold gestures go, repetition speaks volumes, especially in a compact space. There's something so energizing when a pattern—like tufting—recurs in various colors, materials, and scales. The wood tones provide a gravity that helps to ground the room. While it may seem like a stretch to hang a painting on top of a strong pattern, it can be the kind of adventure that's worth the risk.

199

PERSONALITY DRIVEN

There are as many different ways to design and decorate interiors as there people in this world. My favorite spaces are full of personality; they tell the story of the people who live in them. The best offer a real idea of who the occupants are—and what they love.

Furnishings, fabrics, finishes, lighting, art, and accessories: They may be inanimate, but they can and do speak out loud and clear.

Early in my career, I had a passion for French antiques that were aged beyond what anyone could even politely call patina. The gilding was trashed. The wood was chipped. But these pieces had such incredible character. They showed what they were and the lives they'd led. They added so much personality to the rooms where they found themselves. I may have moved on from those old French pieces in style, but definitely not in spirit. They taught me such a great lesson about sticking to my guns and staying away from the expected.

The eccentric, unusual, beautiful things that make us smile, that surprise us, that we fall in love with—these are what reveal us to ourselves and to others. They can be exotic or not. They can be very fine or flea market finds, like those French chairs. Whether kooky, colorful, or really fancy, they're bold, usually one of a kind, and very often witty. Bright colors; large-scale patterns; metallic finishes and bling; shaggy shags, animal prints, and sheepskins; super-overscaled or teensy-weensy—these are the kinds of deliberate choices that make a room personal and delightful. They may not be for everyone, but that is just the point: They lift the spirits of those who are on the same wavelength, and they always infuse a home with life and interest.

ROOMS

PAGE 201: In this double entry, flooring, ceiling details, and chandeliers make it clear that the spaces are related, but unique. PRECEDING PAGES: In the first foyer, the glass leaves on the chandelier presage the living room's pattern play. ABOVE: In a multipurpose room in Arizona, an unusual furniture finish practically blends into the artwork. OPPOSITE: The desk and console set up easily as a bar for entertaining.

One pop of orange energizes this quiet space, which is so rich in pattern. The large canvases (similar, but not identical) by a Chicago-area artist pick up the pattern of the leaded glass in the custom pocket doors, respond to the links in the rug, and confer with the crenelated rim of the tabletop, an antique water-mill gear.

ABOVE: Is there anything more captivating than a cascading constellation of lights sparkling overhead? OPPOSITE: The components of the chandelier pick up on the palette of the antique Indian doors in their gilded frames. In the textural conversation here, the cool-to-the-touch smoothness of the polished concrete tabletop balances the warmth of the hides and the plush, figured rug.

TOUCH ME WITH TEXTURE

Sexy spaces are great. But spaces that wow the eye—and then do more—are far more appealing. These rooms don't just show off their natural attractions. They say: "Come in. Sit here. Get comfortable. Have a coffee or a glass of wine." What actually pull us in are the conversations the objects, materials, and fabrics have with one another. Texture, which I see as pattern in more than one dimension, always plays a major role in these confabs. Life would be so cold and uninteresting without it.

Texture is design's tactile emotional trigger. The touch-me/touch-me-not quality of each surface acts like an on/off switch for the way we respond to and inhabit a room: The more texture and textural contrast, whether subtle or pronounced, the greater our compulsion to touch. I want people to ask: "What is that fabric? What is that feel? What is that made of?" And of course I want them to be so captivated by the different sur-faces that they can't keep their hands to themselves.

In texture, as in color and pattern, there's such a wide spectrum of possibilities. Textiles, in particular, can be barely there, whispery soft, silkily smooth, happily plush, or deliciously shaggy—and everything in between. Each type of weave and fabric construction has its purpose and functional dos and don'ts. Those are always important. But what's truly fascinating is the drama inherent in the contrast. Every texture gains in impact by sharing space with a completely different texture—rather like the flowers in a garden. The gardeners I know pride themselves on both the beauty of the individual species and on the overall effect of the different varieties, shapes, heights, colors, and leaf and bloom sizes that they grow side by side. I've often thought that our interiors are like gardens in that way, so we should cultivate them with those principles in mind.

OPPOSITE, CLOCKWISE FROM TOP LEFT: I am crazy for these antique doors, with their patina of age, saturated color, and intricate metalwork. My pearl-and-jewel-encrusted candlesticks are inspired by Chanel and add fun fashion notes wherever they strut. Each hand-carved, mahogany figure has its own attitude. In the spirit of a midcentury cocktail set, this barware says, "Let's get the party started!"

PRECEDING PAGES: As a statement about mixing eras, this bedroom is emphatic. The two-tone ombré velvet on the early twentieth-century chairs shimmers. Gilded vintage wall art gives the headboard extra height; midcentury bedside tables and a contemporary chandelier bring the brio. ABOVE: We repurposed this nook as a sitting area. The table base incorporates salvaged pieces from the original Golden Gate Bridge. OPPOSITE: Lynn Basa's artworks comment on the color story.

The owners of this Chicago townhouse entertain like crazy, so their dining area has a custom table with a pullout/pop-back-in section that extends the table surface to seat twelve. Artist Anna Wolfson brought her skilled hands to tackle the treatment of this double-height wall. The centerpiece is from a carnival booth.

ABOVE: To create high impact in a compact, neutral space, texture will always do the trick—especially when it's beaded. The silver-beaded window treatment picks up the subtle gleam of the wallpaper's tiny glass accents and the sconces' larger glass whoppers. On a custom base, a prized Buddha presides graciously. OPPOSITE: A closer look at the textural contrasts.

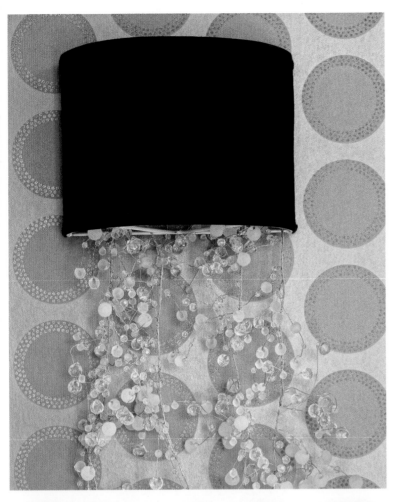

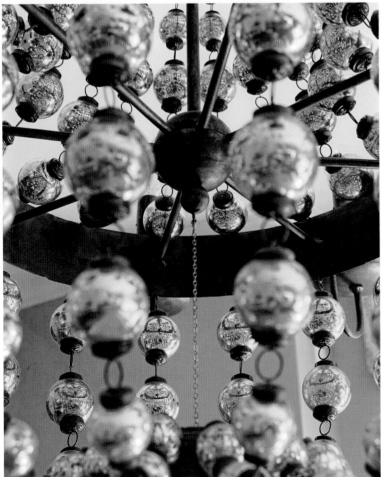

The bead theme continues into the dining area with a chandelier that incorporates gleaming mercury globes. The dining table doubles in size for large gatherings. Comfortable and easy to move, the custom seating embraces the table; perfect for both intimate gatherings and big parties.

In this octagonal room, each of the four "corners" has its own color family. For fun, the Miss Wiggle chairs are dressed like quadruplets: Each wears the same fabric, but in hues that work with its corner's palette. The conversation rondel incorporates three modular units (four would make a complete circle). A variation on the classic French tête-à-tête form, it helps to subdivide the room in an interesting and functional way so all can converse.

COLLECTIONS
AND ACCESSORIES

When people think of collecting, they often imagine serious, focused stalking of expensive, elusive prey. That's one way to look at what a passion for objects and artworks can be, but it's not mine. I encourage a much more relaxed, fun approach, because, in truth, anything from trinket to treasure can trigger our desire to collect.

Accessories can be collections—and vice versa. That's a perspective I took from my fashion background, but it is easy for anyone to see the visceral pleasure that comes from unusual, beautiful, or whimsical things that show personal style. New discoveries, or using familiar items in unexpected ways, can inspire a whole new outlook—and a whole new manner of self-expression.

There are so many different types of objects to fall in love with and display in shelf and tabletop vignettes. Art Deco cigarette cases make me swoon. Miniature crowns (they resemble my logo) call to me like sirens. Vintage sunglasses—the crazier, the better—have such wonderfully kooky charm.

My husband and I love contemporary art, and we collect it together. We found our favorite piece of all in Paris. Surprisingly enough, it's an enormous collage of hundreds of vintage Matchbox cars in a frame that looks like a chrome car bumper. Yes, it has fabulous texture, color, dimension, and scale. What matters to us, though, is its personal meaning. When our son was small, he went through a phase when he wouldn't go anywhere without a Matchbox car clutched in each hand. Every time we look at this piece, it sparks those happy memories.

OPPOSITE: Whether you group your pieces by type, color, shape, texture, material—or you use some other connective thread—be bold. If you organize the pieces in a way that teases out the similarities among the differences, and vice versa, you're bound to please the eye. All these pieces play off the busts at the very center in scale and proportion, while the colors, shapes, and materials balance from top to bottom.

In a huge, eat-in kitchen, muted colors
and quiet materials make sense so as not
to distract from the spectacular views.
Just to give an idea of the scale of the
space, the peacock centerpiece measures
thirty-eight inches from the tip of his
beak to the edge of his tail feathers. The
chandelier, which floats like a horizon
line, is made of patterned pressed glass.

OPPOSITE: When renovating this Victorian mansion in Iowa, we used a high-gloss finish on the restored marquetry floors. This helped to bring the rooms into the twenty-first century and set the stage for gutsy, eccentric, interesting furnishings and artwork. The painting's dimensions comment on the room's proportions. ABOVE: The table base consists of a compilation of vintage and antique industrial chains.

We wanted a rustic piece for the island in our Arizona kitchen, so we brought along the backyard table from our house in Wilmette, with all its great memories. To make the table work for its new purpose, we added eight inches to each leg and covered its faded turquoise boards with a white pearlized paint. The vintage light fixtures, which once hung in a bar, add gorgeous bursts of color.

A POP OF

In our hearts, we all love color—lots and lots of color. Deep. Bright. Bold. Subdued. Surprising. Shocking. Mysterious. Intriguing. Serene. Humorous. Happy. For just about everyone, color means emotion: Its moods cover the spectrum.

Nothing in design is more expressive, individual, and energizing than personal choices regarding color palette. That's why pushing the envelope to make a strong color statement takes confidence. It may be easier to opt for the expected hues and tried-and-true mixes, but it's also a lot less fun.

Sometimes we need to reinvent our color stories. I do. But I also have my lifelong favorites: purple, turquoise, and orange. Purple is royal from way back when, so it connotes richness, stature, and elegance. From eggplant to amethyst to smoky haze to that lavender that's barely there, purple can create a world of magic. Turquoise feels youthful, chic, and sassy—and simultaneously sophisticated and enthusiastic. And orange? It's my crush of crushes.

Color should be an adventure. Selecting and combining shades, tones, and tints—that's risk taking. Look around and find joy in the unexpected variation. Blue and white? Brown and beige? Yellow, red, and green? These are our parents' palettes, and their parents' also. They are also often our own. They endure because they are pleasing, and that's fine. But my aim with color is to help you think about it in a new way, and to use it to surprise, delight, and comfort. So the next time you find yourself attracted to a classic palette, do what I do and change up the foundational shades. Fold in a splash of hot pink or touch of dreamy tangerine, unify with a grounding of black, try on the sophistication that is gray, or go for the command of the royal blues. Suddenly that very nice interior decorated for the everyday becomes fresh, vibrant, and memorable.

There are as many ways to color an interior beautiful as there are colors themselves. The most common include rooms drenched in a single, solid hue; shaded with an ombré of tonal variations; paler than pale with a saturated splash or hot spots here and there; globally warmed with a heat-inspired palette; cooled with an ice-age blend; made epic with the tonal contrast of hot meets cold. Success comes when the hues balance and harmonize across all of the room's surfaces and in all of its three dimensions. Finding the right calculation may take time, but don't overthink it. Have no fear. The best choices may be the most unexpected.

COLOR

PAGE 233: Pops of hot orange and pink sharpen up the serene, cool palette in this master bedroom's seating area.
RIGHT: In some cases, reconfiguring a house's interior architecture can make all the difference for function and aesthetics. Channeling the spirit of northern California in Chicago, we opened up the floor plan and brought in the light with a new glass stair and partial glass wall.

ABOVE: A pair of vintage jacks adds a dash of midcentury modern vigor.
RIGHT: Classic contemporary and midcentury pieces in organic woods and
leather give these rooms a timeless quality. Five groovy glass pendents
over the dining table and embroidered pillows on the sofa work like wake-up
calls on the clean lines and geometric forms of the rest of the pieces.

ABOVE: The shelving unit's angular geometry responds to the rectilinear outlines of its niche. OPPOSITE: There is nothing–*nothing*–quite like the power of lacquer. Maybe it's the high-gloss finish. Maybe it's the quality of the color. But if you want to transform the character of a room to make it extra special and give it an emotional complexity, try lacquering the walls and ceiling in a deep, saturated shade–then enjoy.

ABOVE: "No" is the remnant of a vintage sign found on our travels. With the bar in the Arizona dining room, it creates a juxtaposition that brings a smile. OPPOSITE: The overhead light fixture is an iconic example of Dutch design's new wave, hovering lightly over the midcentury classics: Milo Baughman chairs reupholstered in a favorite color and the always elegant Eero Saarinen dining table.

When a family combines two cultures—
Indian and Chinese—interiors that do the
same seems like the perfect recipe. What
could be a happier, more interesting
marriage of traditions? Their living room
combines the cultural references in a
color palette that calms. With modern
art, one or two pieces of contemporary
furniture, and a silk rug, it's visual Zen.

ABOVE: Turquoise patches in the coffee table's antique-mirror finish reflect some of the tonal variations in the room's palette. An antique tray shows a similar patina. In their marble vessel, I think these iridescent blue eggs resemble Lalique. OPPOSITE: Art sets the stage for the design elements. The upholstery's saffron gold tones and an Asian-inspired lamp layer in more cultural references.

ABOVE: For a gentleman's home office, manly textures and details abound. A side table with a barely-there base balances the solidity of the sofa. OPPOSITE: The dark lacquered walls set the scene for a muted, yet very disciplined, palette that is all about the pleasures of earth tones, blues, high contrast, and the lighter shades of pale. Luxurious textures beckon, and accessories are kept to a minimum.

Plum, deep purple, and teal together—
talk about adventurous palettes and
color explosions. Yet, it works. The
cotton velvets seem to enhance each
hue because of the way the material
reacts to light. Custom pocket doors
with a country French motif add a touch
of history. The antique mirrors that
line the backs of the built-in shelves
help to break up all the white space.

248

ABOVE: For a fashion-lover, a display of draped necklaces adds glamour–and verticality–to a decorative shelf.
OPPOSITE: Making functional use of such a narrow nook requires furniture of just the right proportions.
With their compact, slender, sinuous silhouettes, these pieces fit right in. The profile of this bracelet-like
chandelier has the slim dimensions that make it a perfect solution for a challenging spot.

PALETTE PLEASERS

As FAQs go, the hows and whys of choosing color come high on the list whenever design is being discussed. My own selections always depend on the people and the project. That said, I usually begin with the wall color, which sets the stage for everything else.

For walls, I have a tried-and-trued core palette. These great scene-setters include: white in all its infinite variety, several taupe-y grays, the family of grays from pale to medium to dark, a spectrum of blue-grays, and two particular green-grays. From experience, I've learned these go-to tones align beautifully with every possible color and combination, warm and/or cool, no matter how unexpected.

I love an all-white interior. White walls always look sharp, and they're a great background for colorful modern art and brilliant antique pieces with gilt and silver leaf. To my eye, however, white is a choice that flows from the architectural style of the house. Modern spaces almost seem to demand white. In those interiors where the architectural elements and materials—brick, stone, petrified wood, you name it—provide a great deal of visual texture, white also often proves to be the best complement.

Historic homes and newly built residences inspired by classic European architectural styles often seem to call for more color on the walls. The addition of crown molding or base molding helps to sculpt and craft interiors such as these, and gives them a distinctive personality. A hue on the walls enhances the mood and makes those architectural definitions pop.

Sometimes a special room—an emotional room like a bedroom, library, dining room, or bar—feels ripe for another kind of palette altogether. That's when it's time to set aside the go-to paler shades and opt for lacquered walls in deep, saturated hues, like navy blue and blue-gray. In other words, think outside the paint box and go for drama.

OPPOSITE: For an eight-year-old girl's room, a pink and red palette feels light, bright, and completely right (especially because the colors were her own choices).

ABOVE AND OPPOSITE: For a family who moved from Westlake Village, California, to Chicago, a palette rich in the watermelon and coral hues of the landscape left behind made them feel happy and right at home. Versions of these colors thread their way throughout the house, including in the master bedroom. Dark wood tones and creamy creams, plus a flicker of shine and polished marble, help to balance out the warm, saturated tones.

For a master bedroom in Arizona, a clean, fresh, uncomplicated space seemed just this side of heaven. That meant keeping things on the simple side, so almost everything is white, including the headboard and the original parquet floors, which are lacquered. The effect makes the room appear to float. Cherished vintage Murano millefiori lamps offer grace notes.

NEW

What's better than walking across the threshold of a house with an architecturally significant exterior from another era into a happy, light-filled, modern interior? Houses like these are what I call the "new oldies," and I love them. First, there's always delight in discovering that the inside doesn't—and needn't—match the outside. Then comes the deeper realization that the contrast of design then and now can offer the freshest of all possible worlds, past and present. This has certainly been my experience both as a designer and in my personal life.

When our children were growing up, my husband and I gut-renovated a series of houses on the North Shore that dated from the late nineteenth century to the 1930s. Our goal was always to create a family home that was all about our way of living today, but that also respected history. We delved into our research, learning about architectural origins, period interior styles, and so much more. This proved to be a fantastic design education, since the challenge was to find an informed, inventive way to bring the old up to date.

The most important lesson I want to share with you is this: Never strip away all the historic details. Even if the decision is to demolish the existing structure and rebuild from scratch, it's vital to try to keep and refurbish some, if not all, available elements of the original.

Imagine this scenario, just as a for instance: You've purchased a darling little Tudor from the 1920s, an outbuilding on what was once a large estate, on property where you plan to put up a large, stylish contemporary house. Don't let the wrecking ball do its work before touring the interior, noting the surviving traces of any original finishes and architectural ornament, and photographing as much as possible of the remaining interiors (even with your smartphone). This can provide great inspiration for all the design decisions to come. Even when the plan is to build and furnish the new place entirely from scratch, don't miss the opportunity to salvage and incorporate (or re-create) some of the surviving elements into the new dwelling. In design as in life, everything old can become new again.

OLDIES

PAGE 259: With its details and historical references, this newly built home doesn't look brand-new. For each of the fireplace surrounds, I developed classically inspired profiles, contemporary proportions, custom tile, and mirrored details to enhance the old/new dichotomy. LEFT: Wood-paneled spaces like this Prairie-style living room can feel dark, so even a simple change—like painting the fireplace white—can make a world of difference.

ABOVE: Fresh white walls brighten up a Prairie-style interior that retains all of its original millwork. It's important to be especially careful in choosing accessories and lighting for historic interiors because they can—and should—look modern. OPPOSITE: There may not be any mesmerizingly crazy fabrics here, but those with quiet texture and understated pattern still work their magic within the room's realm.

LEFT: Open, airy, barely-there elements like this chandelier and dining table help to update an architecturally important room. They also add loads of personality. Dining chairs with a slim, tailored profile contribute to the cause, as do a few pops of irresistible turquoise. PAGES 266-267: In the dining and living rooms, many of the details emphasize transparency, clean lines, and uncanny geometries. The violins are vintage

ABOVE: A large, modern sculptural work and modern art carry an elegant antique console and its antique accessories forward into the twenty-first century. OPPOSITE: This two-story family room often makes visitors gasp when they enter. With a twenty-two-foot-high wall, furnishings, art, and accessories must speak to its scale to make their presence felt. Aged objects read clearly against the hand-applied wall covering.

A true find, the turtle-glass light fixture in this Victorian mansion's family room is beautifully iridescent. We needed a sturdy piece and we loved its look, but the dealer wasn't sure of the attribution. When we were getting ready to hang it and peered inside, there it was: Tiffany NYC. Eric Hausman, this book's principal photographer, is also a fine artist; his images have a lovely, mysterious quality printed on stainless steel.

ABOVE: All of these antique stoneware vases share the same glaze but in different states of wear. Arranged on a tarnished antique silver tray, with an occasional flower, the composition of varied shapes and sizes looks and feels just right. OPPOSITE: Earthy touches like a custom fireplace surround with Moroccan-inspired tiles and reclaimed wood bring an organic, multicultural mood to this Chicago interior.

ANTIQUES AND FAMILY PIECES

Every room should include some history, though the reason for this is not the obvious one. Yes, family keepsakes and heirlooms help express personality. Yes, traditional elements like moldings can warm up a stripped-down space. And yes, antiques and vintage pieces always add an interesting visual twist. What's really important, though, is that older items are one of a kind. Their uniqueness jump-starts our curiosity. Where is that piece from? How was it made? What is it about? When something, especially something aged, catches my eye, these are the questions that I ask.

Finding the proper antiques takes ability and experience because "proper" doesn't mean fancy, high-end, or expensive. It means unusual, distinctive, even eccentric—and not afraid to show age and patina. It means searching through thrift stores, garage sales, flea markets, and antiques barns—and better dealers, too—to find something that speaks to you, and fits the spot you want to fill to perfection. (When I can't sleep, I sometimes lie in bed imagining where my latest, characterful discovery is going to go.)

Working with givens—family pieces, favorites, and the like—makes the process of creating a family residence much more enjoyable because everyone gets involved. The best approach to any design, it turns out, is to reinvent the environment—but hold on to its history, too.

OPPOSITE: Transforming an underused front porch into another room for living not only made the space more functional, it gave a family who loves to entertain another area for celebrations. Light, bright, and happy, this new room welcomes all with comfortable seating and other furnishings. Pillows and accessories, including a repurposed Le Creuset Dutch oven, add color and unexpected pattern.

ABOVE: Vintage cutting boards, collected over many years, found the perfect home in this traditional yet modern white kitchen. Both rustic and elegant, they look like—and really are—functional American folk art. OPPOSITE: The area behind the stove is an opportunity to make an art statement.

OPPOSITE: The subtle shimmer of an iridescent malachite wall covering helps move light through this paneled room (and adds some quiet glamour). Its understated pattern responds to the tracery motif on the Roman shades. A pristine white Eames chair and ottoman and the hide rug infuse the room with modern notes. ABOVE: For unexpected texture, there's nothing quite like a hefty piece of modern furniture with a dimensional surface.

OPPOSITE: A backsplash of subway tiles introduces much-needed brightness to the wood-lined kitchen of this Prairie-style house. ABOVE: In a casual dining area in the corner of a converted front porch, an oversize lantern, meant to hang outside, offers a comment on the indoor/outdoor dynamic. Antique Swedish children's-carryalls, each displaying their owners' initials, add their charms to the wall.

ABOVE AND OPPOSITE: A desk on one side of the bed and a nightstand on the other enhance the functionality of this master bedroom and help make it more open. The proportions of the room demand that the individual case pieces be quite large. While the two share an ebonized finish, each has its own carved ornamentation and distinctive details that play into the design of the linen-lined chandelier.

OPPOSITE: Adding a wainscot to a tiny powder room suits the interior architecture of the rest of this home and feels very contemporary next to the mirror's antique gilt frame. ABOVE: A gnarled wood mirror frame comments on the wallpaper's chain pattern, which picks up on details of the original wood paneling.

ACKNOWLEDGMENTS

I am one of the luckiest women in the world! My cadre of family and friends has surrounded me with love each and every day. With my circuitous path to this interior design career, I have gleaned inspiration from absolutely everyone and everywhere. And here's a special high five in heaven to my beloved Irish grandmother Josephine, who will always be front and center in my heart.

My parents, Audrey and John, who raised me with the idea that anything is possible. To this day—and they're both now 91—they encourage me to believe that success comes through hard work, a positive attitude, and lots of laughter. Their love and support have been my rock.

My siblings, John, Mark, and Marcia who taught me how to channel the well-known quality that is sibling rivalry—including the laser-focused desire to have my voice heard at the dinner table always—into strength: You just have to make what you do and say more interesting than anyone else!

Heartfelt gratitude for getting the perfect in-laws as part of my marriage package. Bonna and Donald, you have always been supportive from the very beginning and at no time has that support faltered.

Of course, my divine husband, to whom this book is dedicated. You have shared with me the joy of our three children, Caroline, Alexander, and Madeline. No one ever told me just how profound these relationships would be or that they would just keep getting better and better as they grow older. As their mother, I know that in life they are my true jewels.

As I look back on my career I remember the dynamic women who have inspired me to be strong, independent, and driven. I cannot help but mention two from my days at Neiman Marcus in Chicago. Helen Lewis, human resources manager, who hired me right out of college and placed me front and center at the entrance to the store. She had confidence in me that I later came to realize. Thank you for that crash course! And Amy Steiner, my first department manager, who took me under her wing and taught me about the power of personality and presentation.

Of course, where would I be without my amazing clients?! From my very first adventurous ones, who trusted me when I did not yet have projects or photographs to share and made the beginning seem so very right, to my current lot, who trusts me so implicitly to build the homes of their dreams. To all of you, I am forever grateful and humbled. I learn something new from each of you; from the journey that we share and the mutual respect that drives it and from listening to you and your families as you experience that dose of Modernique®. Thank you all for the beautiful homes that make up these pages.

I have been tickled pink by the work of my brilliant photographers: Eric Hausman, Werner Straub, Eric Prine, Laura Moss, Alan Barry, Marco Ricca, Nathan Kirkman, and, last but not least, Max Kim-Bee. The beauty that you all see behind the camera is an inspiration to continue on in my craft. Photoshoot day is always like a holiday and you make it easy for me to celebrate.

Thank you to my stylist gal pals through the years: Hilary Rose, Diane Ewing, and Barry Leiner Grant. Y'all have the perfect combination of style, hustle, and muscle.

My fabulous Buckingham Interiors + Design team assists me in executing all of this beauty on a day-to-day basis. It indeed takes a village to schedule, coordinate, select, present, share, order, expedite, install, and even clean up a few wayward things along the way. Your energy, enthusiasm, and dedication have propelled me to the heights at which I am lucky enough to be today.

The incredible family and remarkable team members at the Cosentino Group have enriched my horizons over the years in terms of both product development and global travel. Patty Dominguez, my dear friend, I am forever indebted to you for introducing me into your wonderful world.

I would like to thank my treasured licensee partner Global Views for making my product design dreams come true. David Gebhart, Frederick Rayner, and Lois Del Negro: You have all been such a pleasure to collaborate with and the elegance and sophistication that you imbue into all of my pieces has made me so incredibly proud. Thank you, too, to Josh Jarboe, national sales director of Global Views, for your support and that of your über-talented team, who walk the walk and talk the talk of all things Julia Buckingham for Global Views.

Not to forget all of the editors worldwide who have allowed my work to grace the pages of their glorious publications. Thank you so very much to: Diana Bitting, Jaime Derringer, Susan Dickenson, Sophie Donelson, Irene Edwards, Samantha Hart, Laura Hine, Brooke Hubbuch, Pamela Jaccarino, Kerrie Kennedy, Ann Maine, Crystal Palecek, and Jan Parr. I would also like to thank Andrew Martin's *Interior Design Review* for including me in their compendium of the world's greatest designers three years in a row. This truly is the utmost compliment in our business and one of the most thrilling.

My hat is off to all of my supportive and dear colleagues within the interior design community who have shown their love in soooo many ways. The loudest din is the one made by your peers as their voices speak the same language. The people that I play with at all of the national and international design markets warm my heart. As a community, we should be proud of our rock solid relationships and commitment to continuous inspiration. Thank you to the International Market Centers in High Point and Las Vegas for your longtime support and for all of the fantastic speaking and promotional opportunities with which you have enriched me.

Thank you, Nancy Hazlett and Leanne Lawton, my partners in Cincinnati antique shop crime. Our storefront Crackle was my first entrepreneurial adventure and it was a whole lot of fun!

To my publisher, Abrams, I am beyond grateful. You have given me the greatest gift of my career to date and the support of your incredible team has allowed me to realize my long-held dream of creating an inspiring and luscious publication. Thank you from the bottom of my heart for your belief in me and in my work. To the editorial team, you have simply spoiled me for life: thanks to Annalea Manalili, associate managing editor; Danny Maloney, design manager; Denise LaCongo, production manager; and to my editor, Shawna Mullen. What a delight and a joy to work with such true professionals.

Jill Cohen, I can't tell you how over the moon I am that Laurie Salmore introduced me to you as well as to Global Views. Jill, your dedication and perseverance led me to this perfect storm. I will always be in complete awe of your educated eye and the talent that you so modestly downplay. You have inspired me these last couple of years to work harder and to design better! Love, love, love.

To Doug Turshen and David Huang, I feel as if you took a plethora of images and created a magical, sculptural combination where each page grabs you and won't let you go. You made it all seem so easy. What amazing creatives you are. Thank you for everything you do.

To Judith Nasatir, thank you for finding a way to get my thoughts onto paper, in my voice!

My world would not be as beautiful without the support of my beloved vendors in Chicago and around the country. Thank you all beyond thanks, but especially my local go-tos: Oscar Tatosian at Oscar Isberian Rugs, whom I have known since childhood; the ladies of The Find and Redefined Decor; The Fine Line; Maya Romanoff; Jayson Home; Bedside Manor; Scout; The Painted Lady; Heritage Trail Mall; and Josie's.

Special appreciation to my Atlanta treasure, Michelle Bradley of BRADLEY, who created many of the furnishings that grace these pages. Time and time again you have come through for me with gems to fill my client's homes.

*For my husband, John Edelmann, whom I met
and fell in love with in kindergarten. Just goes
to show how your first instinct is usually right.*

Editor: Shawna Mullen
Designer: Doug Turshen with David Huang
Production Manager: Denise LaCongo

Library of Congress Control Number: 2016945924

ISBN: 978-1-4197-2481-7

Printed and bound in the United States
10 9 8 7 6 5 4 3 2 1

Abrams books are available at special discounts when purchased in quantity for premiums and promotions as well as fundraising or educational use. Special editions can also be created to specification. For details, contact specialsales@abramsbooks.com or the address below.

ABRAMS The Art of Books
115 West 18th Street, New York, NY 10011
abramsbooks.com